PREFACE

Photo:
2016 Maker Ed tinkering
workshop at Autodesk,
sponsored by Infosys

" Playing *is* learning,
and when I'm playing,
I don't want to stop."

— RILEY, OPAL SCHOOL 4TH GRADER

Educators are among the adults who, ideally, never stop learning. Since 2012, Maker Ed has had the incredible privilege of providing a variety of workshops for educators, most often in professional development contexts. No two have been the same. As we tinker with our approaches, materials, and tools, we're constantly striving to tailor and refine each experience to the needs of educators and, ultimately, make each experience better. We're continually learning what it means to learn in the most effective and joyful ways possible.

This guide is intended to support your own efforts to provide professional development workshops in tinkering. Throughout, we'll use artbots as the primary project example because we find them to be a great exercise in building skills inherent in tinkering and making, but you can substitute with any other maker activity or project of your choosing. The more important pieces are the context and framing that we provide.

This guide is not intended to be an exacting recipe for your tinkering workshop. Rather, it's meant to be a resource and source of inspiration to support your own ways of providing impactful making experiences.

THE SCOPE OF THIS GUIDE

We begin by sharing a foundation for understanding the terms "tinkering," "making," and "maker education," in a way that's intended to support and provoke discussions in your own workshops. We also focus on ways of empowering all educators to see themselves and their learners as makers and collaborators.

We then move to facilitating workshops, using artbots as an example, including themes to consider, practices, and other considerations when setting up a workshop. Lastly, we provide a suggested format and schedule with practical tips, approaches, practices, and suggested tools and materials. ≡

Maker Ed

TABLE OF CONTENTS

This work was created in part by the entire Maker Ed staff, with specific contribution by Steve Davee, Goli Mohammadi, Lisa Regalla, Stephanie Chang, Jessica Parker and Warren (Trey) Lathe.

MakerEd.org | 🐦 @MakerEdOrg | 📘 /MakerEducationInitiative | 📷 @MakerEdInitiative

The Maker Education Initiative is a non-profit project of the Tides Center, Tax ID: 94-321-3100

INTRODUCTION

What Are Tinkering, Making, and Maker Education?

Tinkering is all about seeing the possibilities of materials through open-ended exploration. It's about making use of playful inclinations and curiosity without imposing prescriptive goals or outcomes. It's a state of play that has tremendous value, even if it doesn't lead to a particular project or product. Tinkering is fundamentally about the process.

At its simplest, making is the act of creating something, whether a poem, a robot, or a cardboard arcade. Making can spur creativity, curiosity, collaboration, and confidence.

Maker education harnesses the power of tinkering and making to create an engaging and motivating learning experience. It's an interactive, open-ended approach that is learner-driven and allows for the time and space needed to develop diverse skills, knowledge, and ways of thinking.

At Maker Ed, we believe that the design of any learning opportunity must recognize and celebrate every learner's ability to experience and influence their world. Maker education can achieve this ideal because it embodies the following core values and goals.

- **Empowerment:** Focus on the learner's capability to voice their unique thoughts, choices, and ideas.
- **Access:** Provide a spectrum of entry points for learners of any culture, background, or ability to take part, and is highly adaptable for educators and learning environments of all kinds.
- **Process:** Include and emphasize exploring, designing, reiterating, reflecting, and sharing as part of the universal process of learning and development.
- **Community:** Welcome and value every learner, as they're encouraged to share, collaborate, and engage with one another.

Maker education allows us to move toward a more comprehensive educational approach that better reflects and incorporates the diverse, complex, and ever-changing nature of our world. Through maker education, youth develop new perspectives, a belief in their own abilities, and a passion for learning. Providing tinkering experience for adults—and especially educators—helps remind them of the power of learning through play, process, and peer-to-peer support. Most importantly, it's never too late to tinker and never too late to learn.

Maker Ed

A Diverse Blend of Philosophies and Practices

The foundations of modern maker education are in the progressive eras of such historical luminaries as John Dewey, Maria Montessori, Loris Malaguzzi, and, more contemporarily, Seymour Papert, to name a few. For more details, we refer you to our Youth Makerspace Playbook chapter on "Approaches and Practices" and encourage some happy Internet searching.

To summarize the pedagogies and approaches developed by the countless progressive and innovative educators that have formed the basis of modern maker education, we briefly introduce the foundational concepts of constructivism and constructionism.

In constructivism, knowledge is constructed out of individual and shared experiences. It's an active, rather than passive, approach, emphasizing learning by doing, discussion, and reflection. Constructionism augments constructivism, advocating that co-construction of knowledge happens most effectively through the construction of tangible things and objects that can be shared. The act of creating a physical object is often a powerful experience, as is producing digital tools such as computer code and media or playing with cultural tools such as language, numbers, and music. Tinkering and making allow for active learning and deep engagement at any age.

In these learning theories and the resulting approaches and practices, educators are facilitators and co-creators of learning. They are guides, rather than sole deliverers of content. Authority is shared, and learners become collaborators not only with each other, but with their educators. Youth are encouraged to take on teaching roles and can, in certain areas, very easily exceed adults in knowledge and skill. Educators are learners as well and are encouraged to be transparent about what they do not yet know; this transparency allows them to model a curiosity and a drive to discover as they share in the experience with their learners.

See this insightful article for more detailed information about constructivism and constructionism.

The remainder of this guide is intended to help you create the most engaging maker-centered workshops possible, to spark excitement in new educators and reignite the passion for teaching in experienced educators. The tinkering workshops you run could be the catalyst that drives educators to positively impact the lives of hundreds or thousands of children. ≡

WORKSHOP OVERVIEW

Goals and Philosophy

Our approach for workshops is to create safe environments that allow for maximum ownership, experimentation, play, discovery, reiteration, reflection, and learning. We hope to model our making approach in education through our workshops, so that educators can develop a greater confidence in making and be inspired to infuse making into their work.

This may require that participants are challenged and may struggle with making and maker approaches, but at the same time, we strive to create a workshop environment where participants feel comfortable in the knowledge that they're supported by their peers and the facilitators. If educators can approach the workshops from their dual roles as both facilitators and learners, the workshops can provide a constructive "high-challenge, low-risk" environment that promotes co-learning and co-creation of knowledge while instilling curiosity and a drive to discover.

Seeking Balance, Sharing Authority

Maker educators are constantly seeking to balance the amount of "knowledge presented" and "knowledge constructed" within a learning experience. But one of the greatest joys in playing with this approach is the freedom it allows; educators can share and celebrate what they don't know as much as what they do know. It's a joy to model curiosity, collaboration, and humility and to stand behind the sentiment of "I don't know, but let's find out together!" Plus, we know that when a learner shares in the teaching, everyone else is often more likely to be engaged and empowered by the example.

Oftentimes, our main workshop goals are to allow educators to:
- Deepen their understanding of tinkering and making and think through how they might apply making within their practice
- Engage in a fun and relaxed but challenging experience that invites play, collaboration, experimentation, and reflection
- Grapple with new materials and rethink familiar materials in contexts that allow for novel uses
- Feel confident that they could run variations of a workshop activity with the materials they have at hand
- Model tinkering, challenge-based, project-based, and inquiry-based approaches
- Promote an ethos of knowledge-sharing in which participants adopt a "learn something, teach something" approach (e.g., with newly gained skills, ideas, and techniques)
- Foster personal connections and awareness between participants, in order to provide for shared networking and bonding

Maker Ed

These goals can be modified and refined depending on the workshop audience, the amount of time available, and the particular topic area of focus.

With these goals in mind, begin your workshop planning making sure to:

o Identify your audience.
o Be clear who will be attending the workshop and, if possible, collect information about the ages of the youth they serve, the context they teach in, and their familiarity and comfort level with maker education.
o Define your goals. Feel free to use the ones outlined here as a starting point. What do you want to absolutely make sure that participants walk away from your workshop knowing? These goals become the basis for your evaluation of the workshop as well.
o Always make sure to include an evaluation as a key way to keep learning and improving the workshop over time.
o Allow time in your agenda for networking and for asking questions.

Artbot Overview
WHAT ARE ARTBOTS?

Artbots are generally electromechanical creations that use motors and batteries to create movement. You may know them by one of their many names: drawbots, scribblebots, doodlebots, wigglebots, or simply drawing machines. By any name, artbots are a wonderful entry point for tinkering. With a limited amount of materials and time, both young and old can find joy from playing with movement, color, and iteration.

The most familiar and archetypical design is an inverted cup with markers taped on it and an attached motor that has been modified to vibrate or gyrate by the addition of an offset weight (see image). While there are kits available for purchase to create artbots, the artbot workshop outlined here encourages the use of your own simple materials combined with LEDs and motors to add complexity and possibilities. This design encourages tinkering, which can lead to new discoveries and inventions.

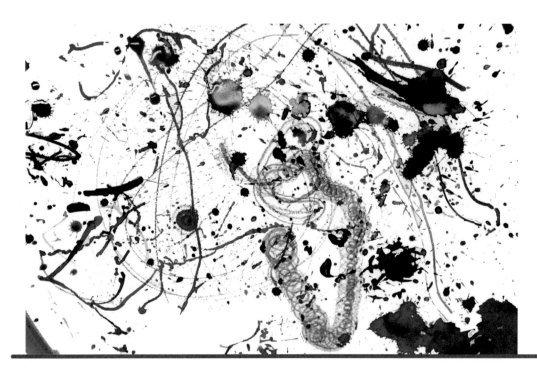

An open-ended artbot exploration can unlock the potential of simple materials and provide just the right amount of challenge. It can enhance a beautiful craft or artistic experience by necessitating engineering and systems approaches. Artbots invite the discovery of concepts such as polarity (most LEDs only work when connected to the poles of a battery in one set direction). They also provide playful opportunities to analyze movement (the direction a motor spins changes according to the order of connection to a battery). Artbot exploration provides a wonderful context to spark curiosity and ask questions about materials and making and to promote complex thinking.

In short, it's all about expanding "What if..." opportunities. Common questions you'll hear include: Where does this battery go? How is it connected? What happens when we add a switch? Where should I put the motor? How about we add a second coin cell? And we invite you to keep (and/or crowdsource) a running list of questions you hear from educators during your workshops.

Artbots typically leave a trace, mark, or impression in their path as they move. The majority of artbots you see in an Internet search show the use of markers, which are convenient for all kinds of artbots. Markers come in a large variety of sizes and colors and are nicely self-contained and reuseable. They're a tried-and-true means of reliably allowing artbots to make their art. Still, they have some potential limitations to consider: They're relatively heavy and large, and cost can add up quickly.

Because these limitations are especially compounded when working with large numbers of workshop participants, we've looked at many ways of using alternatives to markers, any form of "brush" that marks or paints. We found cotton swabs (such as cotton swabs) to be particularly useful in combination with watercolors.

Compared to markers, they:
o   Are cheaper, lighter, and more easily adapted and attached
o   Work well with small vibrating motors that use the same coin cell batteries commonly used with LEDs
o   Allow for smaller, lighter, and less expensive creations using less materials

Another benefit of providing cotton swabs is that they quickly lead people to experiment with other materials for brushes, such as pipe cleaners, feathers, cotton balls, and even painting with UV light and glow-in-the-dark paint! Moving beyond the marker opens up a whole range of other potential "brushes" to be discovered.

It's up to you to decide which materials to provide that can draw, doodle, or make marks. But keep in mind the relationship between the markers, cotton swabs, and brushes and the motors and batteries. Size matters! For example, if you use large brushes, this will affect the kinds of motors and batteries needed for the artbot to move. In Appendix B, we outline some combinations of materials/brushes and motors/batteries that we've used to produce distinct artbot types in previous workshops. ≡

Photo Top Left:
Micro watercolor artbots

Photo Top Righ:
A K'NEX Spinning Artbot

Photo Bottom:
Spinning motion
LED artbot

THE WORKSHOP

Here we provide a sample schedule for a 3–4 hour tinkering workshop as a way to develop some themes and activities a workshop facilitator might consider. The schedule can be adapted to extend the making time or to revisit it at another point during your professional development event.

There are four sections in this sample schedule:
Preparation and Setup
Introducing the Workshop
Facilitating the Activity
Sharing and Reflection

Preparation and Setup

Allow for at least 30–60 minutes to set up all of the materials, tables, and any media you may have. Make sure to have several side tables for supplies. For the tables participants will be using, remember to cover them with heavy poster paper to protect the table surface from marker bleed-through. If liquid watercolor is used, we recommend also having lots of paper towels on hand, as well as ziplock bags to store creations in if they're being taken home by participants. Liquid watercolors provide vibrant painting possibilities but are a bit messy.

Your first consideration is to decide which materials to include based on your budget, the number of participants, and your space. Once you've decided on your materials, you'll want to decide how to lay them out for the participants to use.

We provide a list of suggested materials in Appendix A. You'll want to make sure to choose a variety so that, through exploration and tinkering, participants can build their artbots. For this example project, the motors, copper tape, and batteries are necessary. Part of the reason we've selected artbots using small vibrating motors and CR2032 coin cell batteries is that they tend to be among the least expensive options for motor and battery combinations and require the least amount of supporting materials.

You'll need to factor in the costs and constraints of materials. Motors, batteries, LEDs, and other materials can add up quickly in cost. The decision to invite or require individual, pair, or group work is often dictated by your budget for the workshop. Running a workshop for 50 teachers? Perhaps you can only budget for 25 small vibrating motors that cost $1.40 each. In this case, group work is your friend, and collaboration becomes part of the tinkering and making equation. Remember that you'll always need to keep a few spare motors on reserve for those who might want to take things further or to replace those that break before or during the workshop.

Don't have enough extra materials? Alternate materials can act as substitutes, or you can encourage the focus of the making to shift over the course of the workshop. For example, participants can reuse their initial creations or iterate on their original designs. You can even ask participants to voluntarily bring in materials to share or unique items to contribute. It never hurts to ask, and their contribution can often provide more ownership over the making process and incentive to play with specific materials.

Once you've chosen your materials, intentionally organize and display them in a way to invite discovery and allow participants to work in either groups, pairs, or as individuals. Strive to set a tone of organization, which aids in finding materials, and provides clear places for participants to return them.

Here are some tips:
o Lay out materials neatly over enough physical space so that people can easily access them.
o Provide enough materials, quantity-wise, so that participants can feel comfortable using them but not so much that they feel overwhelmed.
o Provide enough variety so that there's choice, but not so many variations of a single item or multiple items that it overwhelms.
o Take things out of the packaging, so that people aren't automatically dissuaded from using them.
o Include a few surprising items, such as cork, wood, bottle caps, or paperclips; the goal is to use familiar items in unfamiliar ways.
o Provide containers, organizers, labels, or boxes, if they may be helpful.

Nicely presented materials and tools also increase the usefulness of the initial material setup photos for participants. These pictures help record the materials used for later reference, inspire setups in educational settings, and help get participants in the habit of documenting their processes from the beginning.

See Appendix A for examples of the range of materials we've used for maximizing varieties of artbot designs and discoveries. You can get an estimation of quantities from the example setups shown in that section. Keep in mind that you need not provide this full range of materials for artbots. For other types of artbots, you can get away with even less variety and more focused kinds of materials (see Appendix B for more details).

Setup can also be organized dependent on how participants will work together, whether with partners, as individuals, or in small groups. We leave this decision up to you and your materials budget. This workshop can work well with any configuration.

You may choose to invite and emphasize collaboration by encouraging, but not necessarily requiring, working in pairs or small groups of 3–4, which can be subsets of a larger table group of 6–10. Many who prefer to work on their own quickly get involved with others after their initial time of "warming up." Keep an eye out for ways to invite and include participants working on their own, and look for ways to connect them to the larger work.

Educators are very familiar with youth who are reluctant to work with others, or those who do work with others, but in unproductive or disruptive ways. This same problem often persists with adults. They can also have discomfort and anxiety with group work. Acknowledging this and providing the option to work in parallel or on your own is a way to lessen the reluctance to dive in. Often, an invitation to work individually leads to shared experience later. So how do we make pairing and grouping more effective and less potentially painful?

Here are some ideas:
- Self-selection by tables and seating neighbors
- Self-selection by stations
- Pairing by commonality and/or interests
- Random pairings (e.g., find someone you don't know to work with)
- Group by subject matter taught or role in the institution (teacher, coach, etc.)

Introducing the Workshop

Don't underestimate how important it is to start your workshop with introductions and goals for the day. This is your chance to introduce yourself and your organization and to set the tone for the workshop. Be sure to outline your goals for the day and what you hope everyone will walk away knowing and feeling. This is also an important time to inform folks of essentials such as food/snacks, restrooms, access to Wi-Fi, breaks, photo release forms, etc. We always encourage the use of an ice-breaker activity in place of just going around the tables and saying names.

As we shared in our workshop goals, a central theme is how material use can maximize possibilities. Here, the words you use to present the materials can also serve to either limit their potential or open it up. Selecting and setting up materials with careful presentation can be a creative and fun process that helps inspire energy and excitement for making and tinkering. We hope you have fun with it and consider it as important as the language you use to introduce the workshop.

LANGUAGE FOR OPEN AND GUIDED MAKING

A simple tip for using language to maximize the variety of potential designs is to say the least you can while still clearly communicating possibilities. At the outset of a workshop, the amount of information that you share and the expectations you set in introducing the materials has been shown to have a direct influence on the variety of outcomes. The more you say that is inviting, the more possibilities are likely to be discovered and unlocked. While true for many participants, it's not always the case for all. There are considerations for those who expect or prefer more direction and guidance. Fortunately, there are many ways to support the full spectrum of comfort with degrees of guidance and expectations.

Among the many questions that invite open-ended exploration of materials and creation, we often start with:
- What is possible with these materials?
- What might they do and become?

Note that we intentionally don't say: "What can you do with these materials?" or, in regard to artbots, "Using these motors and batteries, create something that makes and/or is art." These questions steer the exploration towards a particular challenge, rather than providing an invitation.

Depending on your goals, you may choose to introduce artbots as a challenge or in a variety of other ways, as illustrated in the two examples below.

Themed or open-guided, electromechanical art invitations:
 "I invite you to create something that makes and/or is art."

Open-narrative stories, character:
 "Create a character and tell a story using the materials provided."

The language used is personal and dependent on the audience—and it's hard to get it exactly right! As we'll discuss throughout this chapter, we have a balance to achieve and ways of course-correcting throughout the workshop. So, while initial words are important, feel free to make them your own, tinker with them, and trust that you'll always come up with new ways to fine-tune the learning experience.

To help put these ideas together, here are some sample workshop opening invitations for you to adapt.

 "In this workshop, we'll explore ways of using the motion of small vibrating motors, LEDs, coin cell batteries, and the materials you see. How might these materials make and/or be art? For example, how might the motion of the motors create drawings, doodles, or art on the paper? As one possibility, we've provided cotton swabs and watercolors. We encourage you to play with a variety of ways that other materials might also make art—through movement, drawing, sound, or using the light of LEDs."

 "I'll leave it to you to discover for yourselves and help each other to get the motor and LEDs working. Look around and ask for help, if needed, from your peers or any of us running the workshop."

 "I'm specifically not showing an example in order to help maximize the variety of designs that you may discover. However, I do have some examples to show if you are absolutely stuck and would like to see them for inspiration. You'll also see examples emerging among your peers, so you'll likely not need mine."

 "Making is all about exploration and messing around. What you discover and create with the materials along the way is every bit as valuable as any actual artbot or other creation. We encourage you to seek and share examples of "serendipitous fits." If what you make doesn't happen to work perfectly, you can consider it a prototype that shows what might be possible with more time. Things need not be fully—or at all—functional to represent your ideas and spark others."

What Is a Serendipitous Fit?

The concept of serendipitous fits is based on the combination of lucky happenstance (serendipity) and fitting (when various parts are being tested and fit together in an effective and often surprising way). Often, unexpected perfect fits occur, with friction and size coincidence holding things together instead of any sort of tape or glue. By inviting their discovery in tinkering, as with tinkering motifs, you can spark new ways of constructing and creating. These inventions and accidental discoveries are made possible by the inclination to take a risk, test, and try new things. They often result from things that aren't working as planned.

Photo: Compilation of serendipitous fits

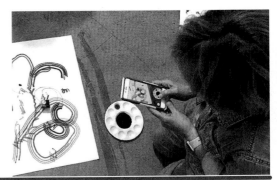

A great instance of serendipitous fitting is illustrated by elementary teacher Maureen Frews, a Maker Ed workshop participant who discovered a new and clever way to connect Lego bricks and cotton swabs for small adaptable artbots. By placing a motor on top of two Lego bricks and paint-drenched cotton swabs in the holes underneath, she was able to create an artistic and fun "fit" for her bot.

EXAMPLES AND DEMONSTRATIONS

In introducing tinkering workshops, especially artbot workshops, we don't usually show examples. This differs from the approach of many workshops that show one or more examples of projects in advance. Instead, we're aiming for variety and less bias in design. However, we do offer to show examples if requested by those who are curious, need clarification, or are simply stuck. We recommend keeping a wide variety available. An example of the language we might use is:

"I have examples of various types of artbots I'm happy to show you if you're truly stuck or even if you prefer to replicate existing designs. While our hope is that you discover new possibilities and try new things, we recognize that there is utility to reverse-engineering designs, and working toward a certain finished product can be a good way to gain comfort with the materials and concepts."

Another approach is to have examples on-hand and around the room that participants can discover rather than calling particular attention to them. We also recommend including examples of non-working and unfinished artbots. These show a range of outcomes and emphasize the process rather than the product. An unfinished artbot or a non-working prototype can be an effective starting place for those who are having a hard time getting started. Perhaps offer, "Would you like to adopt and work on this artbot?"

The goal is to "prime the pump" of ideas by showing a bare minimum that helps people get started. That is, you don't want to show every step of the process. Instead, leave the door wide open by including questions. For those who are unfamiliar with motors, battery connections, and circuits in general, we suggest offering to help individually after a period of experimentation and discovery. Encourage peer-to peer support in this area as well. If a participant can help in your place, that's the preferred option.

You should also join in as well. This is a great time for you to introduce new possibilities and inspire new directions. Feel free to tinker with materials yourself!

Facilitating the Activity

After the introduction, give a full 60–75 minutes for folks to tinker and explore. We suggest building in the option for a "bio break" at any time and encourage the idea of playing music during this time to invite a more playful atmosphere. During this time, you may roam around and take on various roles to support, encourage, and guide tinkering explorations.

There are many roles for you to play during the workshop. In this section, we look at the ways you can guide even the most reluctant participants toward confidence and comfort with making. While many participants will jump right in and need little support, it's fairly common that some will need further support and encouragement.

MEETING RESISTANCE AND RELUCTANCE

Most often in our workshops, we give a brief introduction to the materials, an invitation to explore and play with possibilities, and then set everyone free to begin. Most dive in after looking at and gathering materials. Some run with ideas right away. And some sit still, waiting and unsure of what's expected.

Many adults are rarely invited or "allowed" to play without the pressures or obligations of a specific outcome. Their prior experiences have made them more comfortable with following instructions, seeing examples, and knowing what's going to happen in advance. It's extremely important to honor this reaction. At times, it may be intimidating for some to see others joyfully jumping right in. Some might even feel discomfort or inadequacy as they sit and compare their comfort levels with the active responses around them.

Providing an opportunity to make in a professional development setting is a powerful way to connect the importance of playful approaches with learning and can help educators connect making and open-ended approaches to learning. From the very beginning, acknowledge the disparate levels of comfort with open-ended invitations. Have examples and partial examples on hand. Set the tone that it's more than okay to not get started right away. It's actually very powerful to observe and gain inspiration before starting. The most important thing is for those who are hesitant to have the opportunity to be inspired by their peers.

The vast majority of the time, resistance gives way to not just increased comfort but outright innovation. A mind that doesn't engage right away in materials is often one that's already tinkering with possibilities mentally, taking in what's around, and assessing options. Professional development environments benefit from the diversity of these comfort levels.

Finally, when acting to support someone, ask yourself: Is what I'm saying an inspiration or expectation? An invitation or obligation? These differences can go a long way toward creating more comfort. Above all, "No hurry, no worry."

Most of the time, it'll be the energy and the peers that help reluctant folks eventually get started. But if more effort is needed, there are some simple things to encourage, show, and try that may help:
o   Share an example in progress.
o   If asked, share a complete example.
o   Encourage looking around and reassure that it's okay to start slow.
o   Invite documentation support. Taking pictures helps them look around.
o   Showcase a small, unfamiliar skill, such as stripping a wire.
o   Provide an opportunity to take something apart.
o   Invite writing and drawing.
o   Provide an easier starting place, such as a station with less and simpler materials. LEDs are often a great material for this.
o   Start with familiar art and craft materials and a comfortable thing to make, such as an origami creation.

UN-WHELMING THE OVERWHELMED

It's extremely common for participants to be simply overwhelmed by all the materials and choices. Alternately, they may be heavily invested in getting something to work and simply be stuck. For this reason, we provide a large range of possible materials, multiple starting points, and some reassuring language along the way:

> "Dead-ends happen. Please share them if you can, as they can always represent the seed of new ideas, serve as motifs, and help show the process and your thinking."

> "There's a great benefit to seeing and sharing what didn't work. Seeing how something doesn't work can provide an even deeper understanding of how it does work."

As a setup variation to this artbot workshop example, you may choose to provide additional options designed to support different entry points into tinkering. Particularly for groups that have a wide range of experience in making with motors and LEDs, providing multiple stations of increasing complexity helps. See our setups in Appendix B for examples of LED-only, LED paper circuit, paper only, and various other subsets of materials. Also, if you have the full range of materials, you may consider holding some in reserve and drawing on them as you perceive a need.

When making and project work is in full swing, participants are driving the energy in the room, freeing you, as the facilitator, to roam. However, there's still much you can do to keep the process moving, fun, and effective, as we address in the next few sections.

BREAKING BOTTLENECKS

Best practices in facilitation also include the use of some direct ways of easing past points of struggle and frustration. Instruction, examples, and demonstration of skills, as well as subtle nudges to support and help are all tools you can use. The goal is to remove bottlenecks and points of frustration that are blocking further tinkering discoveries. Keep an eye out for frustrations that are based on things broken, missing, or misused.

Some examples:
o   Noticing a battery is dead and helpfully substituting one in its place.
o   Providing the right tool for the job when the use of a non-optimal one is hindering progress. For example, noticing the need for Torx screws or a better size of Phillips screwdrivers. The right tool is also far safer!
o   Suggesting a better tape to use or a more robust connection method.
o   Keeping an eye out for non-obvious electrical shorts (for example, batteries with connections that connect the terminals or sides of a coin cell directly rather than having a complete circuit that goes through motors or LEDs).
o   Noticing and correcting the wrong battery for the wrong motor. Coin cells are fine for small vibrating motors, but they won't drive larger motors salvaged from printers, for example. A 9-volt battery might help with that.

Maker Ed

A fun role to play as facilitator is that of materials and tool seed-planting. For example, someone might be struggling in a way that just the right tool or material can move them forward. Or an awesome idea might be empowered as it emerges with an infusion of a handy part. One method that works for both youth and adults is to leave a potentially useful material or tool on the table for discovery without comment. Another is to purposefully introduce it with the reason you're doing so: "I saw you struggling with _____ and saw that this binder clip was effectively used by_____."

MORE SOCIAL ENGINEERING: SKILL AND CONCEPT DISSEMINATION

Just as you can stoke creativity and possibilities with tools and materials, so can you by fostering peer-to-peer support and inspiration. View yourself as a facilitator of connections between participants. This can help to elevate the knowledge in the room and support you in breaking bottlenecks. If a participant has experience with Torx screws, perhaps have her share this knowledge with specific participants. If batteries seem to be causing confusion and frustration, ask if anyone in the rooms has experience with different kinds of batteries and wouldn't mind sharing their prior knowledge. This can help to empower participants and create connections.

In your room-roaming, you may notice multiple instances of struggle to tackle the same problem, or complementary projects that might be interesting combined or developed in parallel. Skills are another thing to be on the look out for. A fantastic way to reinforce skills and further empower what has recently been learned is by taking someone who has struggled and succeeded with learning to wire a motor or LED and asking if they would mind helping others out if needed.

Sample language:

"This is something I wasn't going to bring out because of limited quantity, but I have this old camera that might contain useful parts for what you're working on."

"I've seen a bit of a bottleneck at the hot glue station. Would you care for some Glue Dots for those feather attachments?"

"I noticed that you've become very skilled at ____. Would you be willing to help others with that if needed?"

Some things might be worthy of calling attention to for the entire group, especially if they help to introduce new things that you may or may not have already planned to introduce. It's almost always better that this information come from the group! Feel free to be transparent about it: "I was going to introduce this method of connecting clip leads to batteries using these small magnets later on, but ____ has discovered an even better way than I intended. Take a look!"

Remember to stop and highlight a discovery, innovation, resource, or skill and ask participants to share their know-how with others. Encourage peer-to-peer support whenever possible.

Once participants are more comfortable with experimenting, it may be useful to show vibrational motion versus simple spinning and invite a variety of responses to the different motions. Ask, "How are these motors the same? Different? How else might the motor's motion be used?" or "How might the motion be changed?" There are many variables to change and nuggets to be discovered simply by playing with the motors. What happens when you change the length of the rotating arm, add weights, or place the weight in various locations? All options can greatly affect the behavior of the artbot— even the motor position on the artbot itself.

Be approachable for help if someone is struggling. If they need help, make it interesting and show just enough that they can take over as soon as possible. Try not to just provide a solution. Keep them curious, supported, and empowered.

DOCUMENTATION

Documentation is an important component of the making process. It's a way to show attention, capture the process, and let participants know that what they're doing is valued. Documentation in photos, video, audio, and writing become priceless assets when planning future workshops or even when developing guides like this one!

It's powerful to ask adults and youth alike, "Do you mind if I take a picture of what you've made/discovered here to share with others? I'd love to use it to provide inspiration and ideas."

Documentation also allows you to capture and learn things about the process that you may otherwise miss. Our number one tip is to take as many pictures as possible. You can narrow down to a few "keepers" afterward, but you may regret missing something if you keep the camera in your pocket most of the time. And before the workshop begins, be sure to take pictures of the materials, tools, and setups that you use.

The workshop participants should also be invited to document their process. It might be helpful to set up a social media hashtag ahead of time so participants can post and tag their creations online. Another option is to create a sharable folder (via Google or Dropbox , for instance) where participants can upload their images and videos. You can then even set up a rotating slideshow throughout the activity or during breaks. Another option is to have participants text their assets to a specific number for easy curation. The goal here is not to make documentation and sharing complicated but to allow participants to share their processes and creations and to use these collective assets as potential entry points for reflection and growth.

General photo documentation shot list:
- Setups and material presentations in use
- Wide room shots
- Close shots of hands making

Alternately, hand a camera to one of the participants and rejoice in seeing things that you would never think to capture—especially close up. Bear in mind, though, that there is a danger in spending too much time behind the lens looking for the perfect process pictures. Make sure to remind yourself and your participants to set aside the camera and ask questions.

Everyone should be invited to listen in on interactions or use a notebook to write down observations and quotes. Capturing words and interactions throughout the workshop is a wonderful way to document emotions, insights, ideas, and even challenges. You'll see and document the workshop in ways that the camera alone cannot capture.

Sharing and Reflection

Workshop experiences are made more powerful and meaningful through allotted time to share and reflect. Allow time for everyone to present their creations and tinkering results for smaller groups, and perhaps have a "gallery walk" for larger groups (over 10), where portions of the group take turns wandering around the tables and seeing the creations of others. Your decision on gallery walk versus individual sharing will depend on the time you have at the end of your session.

We also recommend allowing time for reflection to take place in small groups for at least five minutes and then opening up discussion for the entire group. While we do provide some guiding questions below, often, the best questions for reflection will emerge from your own observations during the workshop or from the questions, struggles, and triumphs you observe during the tinkering process. The reflection process will be even more valuable and personal for you and your participants if you share your own questions and invite questions from participants.

SAMPLE REFECTION QUESTIONS

o   What was initially challenging, and what became easier?
o   What role did collaboration play?
o   Did you work with others? How?
o   How did your project change over time? What changed about the design and construction?
o   What questions would you ask of your students throughout the process?
o   What additional materials might you include? Tools? What might you leave out?
o   What standards can you connect to this process? What subject-specific vocabulary might you be able to use? (Examples include Brownian motion, oscillations, frequency, environmental adaptation, and other physical and life science concepts and vocabulary.)
o   How might you expand and highlight additional ties to standards and concepts?
o   How might this turn into a long-term exploration?
o   What surprised you about the experience today?
o   Who did you meet that inspired you to try something new?

And importantly, "What are you able to take back and try at your institution immediately?" This is a great question to get the participants thinking of how they might implement what they learned at their own institutions.

Finally, make sure there's time for participants to fill out a brief evaluation to give you feedback on their experience, so that you might incorporate takeaways in future workshops.

CLEANUP

An essential part of any tinkering and making process is cleaning up, so invite everyone to join in! You'll want to allow between 20–40 minutes for cleanup. During this time, perhaps suggest that participants share their tips and tricks for getting youth to clean up. Ask: What are ways that you invite your colleagues or students to clean up? What fun and creative tactics do you use? What incentives seem to do the trick? What insights can you share?

To cut down on costs and impact to the environment, you'll want to reuse parts, so make sure to organize trays, bowls, or stations so participants know where individual pieces and parts should go. You may even choose to have participants take apart their own creations and return materials, separated by material type. ☰

Maker Ed

CONCLUSION

The best way to prepare for your workshop is to take time to play with the ideas and materials presented here, and to combine them with your own. Start by tinkering with whatever materials you have on hand, and taking what you have and don't have as equal creative inspirations. Try prototyping your own artbots with your mix of materials and see what works best for you. Recruit friends and colleagues before planning. Better yet, try these ideas with youth, and be amazed at all that they come up with to stoke your workshop plans.

Our workshops goals go well beyond a hope to spark transformative tinkering experiences for educators. By providing a good mix of fun, creative provocations, and intriguing materials and tools, we wish to help strengthen your own creativity and confidence as well as that of your workshop participants. We welcome you to the family of maker educators. We believe your very interest in this guide strengthens us all and helps to bring more equity of access to maker education.

When we see every single child as a maker, with talents and gifts worthy of being discovered, encouraged, and nurtured, then the possibility of moving toward a more comprehensive educational approach through maker education is achievable. Through making and tinkering, educators and youth develop new perspectives, a belief in their own abilities, and a passion for learning. We see you as a powerful maker, with powerful abilities to change lives.

We hope that by using materials that are relatively affordable, and often re-useable, workshops will become less work and more play. Tinkering and making are joyful ways to learn. We can't wait to learn from your own artbot innovations, tinkering revelations, and findings of serendipitous fits. Share your inspirations and insights with us online by using the #makered hashtag via social media or feel free to email us at PD@makered.org. ☰

APPENDIX
Maker Ed Resources Appendix

Professional Development:
- Free online, self-paced PD modules, on topics including why making matters and tinkering
- Micro-credentials to help guide educators towards the acquisition of research-backed, expert-assessed skills or competencies on specific maker educator tasks, including choosing materials that matter, creating learner driven curriculum, and documenting and reflecting on making

Documentation and Open Portfolios Project:
- General information on our Open Portfolio Project
- Publications (free PDFs) including Research Briefs from Phase I and the Practical Guide to Open Portfolios
- Hard copies of the Research Briefs and the Practical Guide

Online Community:
- Maker Ed's Twitter and Facebook feeds showcase and link to great communities and resources for maker educators
- Maker Ed's Google+ community might also prove helpful

Other Resources:
- Maker Ed's Youth Makerspace Playbook, available as a free PDF or for purchase as a hard copy
- Maker Ed's Resource Library includes both Maker Ed and external resources for a wide range of maker education needs
- Maker Ed's blog highlights our work, as well as other maker education work we're excited about
- Join the Maker Promise, a collaboration of Maker Ed and Digital Promise, funded by the Moore Foundation. Maker Promise is a community resource for schools and school districts around the country to start and build their maker education programs.

Maker Ed

MATERIALS & TOOLS SUGGESTION LIST

The beauty of artbots is that you can make them from almost anything. Here is our list of favorite materials and tools to have on hand. Wherever possible, try to offer various sizes and colors of a material.

MATERIALS MADE OF WOOD	Spools Craft dowels Wooden buttons Toothpicks	Clothespins Coffee stir sticks Popsicle sticks, colored and natural	Corks, synthetic and natural
MATERIALS MADE OF METAL	Binder clips Metal brads	Paper clips Wire	Safety pins
CRAFT/ART SUPPLIES	Watercolor palettes and/or liquid watercolors	Brushes Feathers Googly eyes Pipe cleaners	Small fabric squares Rubber bands Hair bands Cotton swabs
MATERIALS MADE OF POLYMERS	Straws Plastic spools	Zip ties (especially small sizes)	Sections of pool noodles Bits of polyethylene packing foam

TYPES OF PAPER	Origami paper	Paper stir sticks	Squares of chipboard
	Post-It notes	Cardboard	

CLIP LEADS	Vibrating motors, one per person, pair, or small group		

TYPES OF TAPE AND GLUE	Masking/labeling tape	Glue dots	
	Duct tape	Electrical tape	

TOOLS	Scissors	T-handle reamer (makes holes larger)	Small hacksaw
	Awls	Hole punch	Needlenose pliers
	Drills with step bits	Electrical diagonal cutters	Wire cutters
	Heavy duty cutters/shears	Wire strippers	Bowls or holders for magnetic parts
	Small hobby saw		

There are many different ways to organize materials for the participants, including on each table, on individual place settings, or in a centrally located area for all participants to pull from.

APPENDIX B

ALTERNATIVE ARTBOT TYPES AND MATERIALS

Artbot design possibilities are greatly influenced by material selections. To help you think about which materials to use for your workshops, we share examples of artbot types developed from some more specific materials and constraints. For each artbot type, we share the motors, batteries, and "brushes" that we most commonly use.

All of these suggestions can, of course, be changed, combined, and played with. We encourage you to tinker with each type and discover more. Whatever materials you decide to start with for your workshops, it helps to play with them in advance to get an idea of how well they work and what may be missing that could allows the greatest potential flexibility and effectiveness of the materials.

FOAM AND MARKERS
Motors: Vibrating toothbrush motors
Batteries: AA cell
Brush: Markers

This super simple artbot is a variation of the archetypical inverted cup with taped-on markers. Instead of a cup and tape, it uses a length of pool noodle (HDPE foam) and rubber bands. The motor in this example is salvaged from a dollar-store electric toothbrush, leaving the battery holder and switch mechanism intact while exposing the vibrating motor. All of these parts are easy to build off of and can be reused. The foam can be easily cut and used in any configuration, providing much variety beyond the simple example shown here.

RECYCLED MATERIALS
Motors: Small hobby DC (typically 1.5V)
Batteries: AA or C cells
Brush: Markers

This artbot variety is most closely related to the typical inverted cup model. In our approaches, we encourage a wide range of recycled materials in any configuration. The motors used in this example are great for use with cups, bottles, pieces of cardboard, and packing materials. Typically, these artbots are easily made with tape and do not need hot glue, though hot glue can be useful for allowing a greater variety of designs.

MICRO-WATERCOLOR
Motors: Small vibrating motors
Batteries: CR2032 coin cells or LR44 button cells
Brush: Cotton swabs
This artbot is the primary example we use in this guide, repeated here for comparison purposes. It's an approach that makes use of a wide variety of the materials we've shared. The "micro" comes from using tiny 6mm vibrating motors, cotton swabs, and watercolors to make artbots that paint as they move. Because of their small size and ability to make use of the widest range of materials types, these artbots have been among the most varied and interesting.

HDPE FOAMBOTS
Motors: Small vibrating motors
Batteries: CR2032 coin cells or LR44 button cells
Brush: Cotton swabs or pipe cleaners
In this variation, there's one main material that allows for a large variety of designs: high-density polyethylene foam, or HDPE, which can be rescued from the landfill and put to use for easily constructed and infinitely adaptable micro-watercolor artbot designs. These can be constructed without the need for glue or tape, making them another option for reusable and easily workable materials that don't depend on tools (although scissors are handy).

LEGO BRICKS
Motors: Small vibrating motors
Batteries: CR2032 coin cells or LR44 button cells
Brush: Cotton swabs
Lego offers some convenient dimensions that allow for serendipitous fits. Cut cotton swab ends fit in the small holes on the bottom of Lego plates, allowing for very small artbots held together entirely by friction. With some slight modifications of hole size, 6mm vibrating motors can also be nicely incorporated within Lego creations. Also, 5mm straws fit within the 4.8mm Lego holes, opening up even more design options.

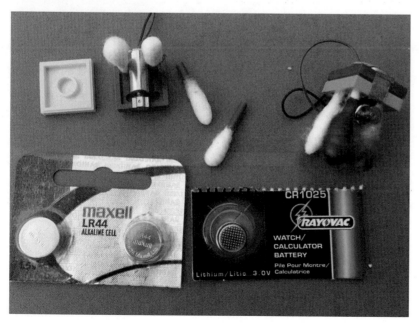

Lego Artbot Materials
For a table of 5-8 participants:
    Rolls of colored label tape (2–3)
Pairs of scissors (4–5)
Coin cell batteries, CR2032 (10)
LEDs, various colors (20)
Pieces of HDPE foam (5)
Straws of various sizes (20–30)
Pipe cleaners (10–20)
Zip ties
Binder clips of various sizes
Brass brads of various sizes
Cotton swabs (30–40)
Watercolor pallets (2)
Popsicle sticks of various sizes (20)
Various small wooden buttons, dowels,
    and clothespins

K'NEX CONSTRUCTION SETS
Motors: 1.5V DC or 9V cassette tape motors
Batteries: AA cell or 9V
Brush: Markers

The use of K'Nex is a wonderful way to allow for continual rebuilding and experimentation with artbots. An added bonus is that the creations are actually rather robust, and no glue or tape is required. Multiple motors and batteries can easily be added, leading to some surprising and interesting movements and behaviors. These artbots can work with small DC motors, including the electric toothbrush vibrating motors, but they work especially well with high-voltage cassette-tape motors. It's very simple to connect the terminals of the 9V battery with the motor using clip leads.

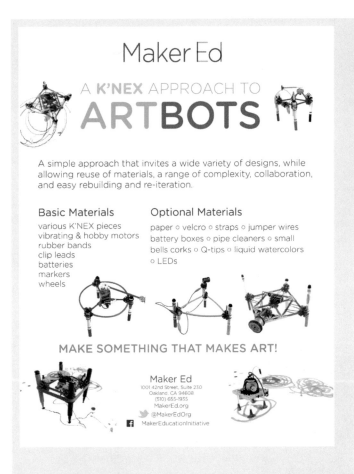

Maker Ed

A **K'NEX** APPROACH TO
ARTBOTS

A simple approach that invites a wide variety of designs, while allowing reuse of materials, a range of complexity, collaboration, and easy rebuilding and re-iteration.

Basic Materials
various K'NEX pieces
vibrating & hobby motors
rubber bands
clip leads
batteries
markers
wheels

Optional Materials
paper ○ velcro ○ straps ○ jumper wires
battery boxes ○ pipe cleaners ○ small
bells corks ○ Q-tips ○ liquid watercolors
○ LEDs

MAKE SOMETHING THAT MAKES ART!

Maker Ed
1001 42nd Street, Suite 230
Oakland, CA 94608
(510) 655-1935
MakerEd.org
@MakerEdOrg
MakerEducationInitiative

Maker Ed
Every Child
a Maker

A **MICRO WATERCOLOR** APPROACH TO
ARTBOTS

A simple approach that invites a wide variety of designs, while encouraging reuse of materials, a range of complexity, collaboration, experimentation, and iteration.

Basic Materials
Vibrating pager motors
coin cells CR2032
Recycled High density polyethylene foam (HDPE)
Q-tips
liquid watercolors, solid water color pallets, or food coloring

Source examples
evilmadscientist.com
batteriesandbutter.com
packaging, pool noodles

Art stores

Optional Materials
paper ○ wire ○ pipe cleaners
small bells ○ corks ○ LEDs
office supplies ○ craft
materials ○ LEGO ○ KNEX
copper tape ○ dollar store
electric toothbrushes

Tools
Only scissors needed!

How might these materials make and/or become ART?

APPENDIX C:
MATERIALS ORGANIZATION

Pictured here is an example of a Table Possibility Box, just one way of organizing and laying out materials for participants to use. Origami paper is a very useful material that can also be used as a nice design accent. Color can be an inspiration! This amount of materials easily serves about 8-10 educators.

Photo:
Common materials distributed to each table.

Photo: Table supplies equally distributed (USPTO Dallas)

Photo:
Materials sorted and staged in advance for table distribution

Maker Ed

SAMPLE 3 1/2-HOUR WORKSHOP AGENDA

8:30–9:00
Arrival and check-in

9:00–9:15
Welcome and introductions

9:15–10:45
Exploration and creation with materials; includes clean up and showcasing creations on table

10:45–11:00
Break and gallery walk, where participants informally walk around and notice the materials used and the overall creations

11:00–12:00
Reflections, where participants share in large group or break up into smaller groups to discuss.

Reflection questions:
1. What did you notice about your own process? For example, emotions, interest in materials, focus, work style (independent/collaborative, etc.).
2. What did you notice about your peers' process/creation/use of materials?
3. What role did collaboration play?
4. How might this turn this activity into a long-term exploration?
5. What surprised you about the experience today?
6. Who did you meet that inspired you to try something new?

For educators interested in standards:
1. What standards can you connect to this process? What subject-specific vocabulary might you be able to use? For example, Brownian motion, oscillations, frequency, environmental adaptation, and other physical and life science concepts and vocabulary.
2. How might you expand and highlight additional ties to standards and concepts?
3. What are you able to take back and try at your institution, school, library, etc. immediately? Potential prompt: "I would be crazy if I went back to my institution, organization, classroom, etc. and didn't _____(fill in the blank)."
4. What are some challenges to consider when applying this activity to your classrooms, schools, libraries, etc.?